Traction Engines
& Recollections

Garrett of Leiston

CW00663836

NO 1186

Contents

Frontispiece: **STANWAY** *Mercury* attends the Gloucestershire Warwickshire Railway Steam & Vintage Gala at Stanway House in October 2001.

© Malcolm Ranieri, 2011

Photos: © Malcolm Ranieri, 2011

All rights reserved. No part of this publication may be reproduced, stored in a retrieval system or transmitted, in any form or by any means, electronic, mechanical, photocopying, recording or otherwise, without prior permission in writing from Silver Link Publishing Ltd.

First published in 2011
British Library Cataloguing in Publication Data
A catalogue record for this book is available from the British Library.
ISBN 978 1 85794 373 3

Introduction

The firm of Richard Garrett & Sons Ltd has a long and varied history. The first Richard Garrett set up as a bladesmith in Leiston, Suffolk, in 1778, and it was his grandson, also Richard Garrett, who commenced the manufacture of steam engines from 1830. However, these early machines were fixed, and the firm also made farm equipment such as seed drills, ploughs and threshing machines.

The first portables were built in 1848, followed in the late 1850s by the first agricultural traction engines, under licence at first, then from 1876 to Garrett's own design. Garrett also built other forms of steam-powered engines in late-Victorian times: road rollers of all sizes, ploughing engines, and road locomotives for heavy haulage, some of which became showman's engines. The company also exported its engines to Europe and the colonies, especially New Zealand.

From 1905, due to changes in legislation regarding road haulage, Garrett produced its attractive and versatile model 4CD steam tractor, which was very popular for local authority and contractor light haulage work.

The company also built steam wagons in various forms from 1909 to 1930; nearly 1,000 were produced during that time, of which four have been preserved. An experiment prior to the First World War, to combat the internal-combustion-engined tractor, was the lightweight steam tractor known as the 'Suffolk Punch', after the heavy draught horse; although it was not successful, one has been preserved.

This very versatile company diversified from steam to manufacture electric vehicles, refuse vehicles, Army vehicles, all forms of agricultural machinery, machine tools, and many other engineering products. As the use of steam declined, Garrett joined an amalgamation of steam manufacturers called Agricultural & General Engineers, and when it collapsed in 1932 the family firm of Richard Garrett & Sons died with it. Around 22,500 steam engines had been built, the majority being portable engines, and around 120 have been preserved; the company's 'Long Shop' factory at Leiston has been restored and is now the Garrett Museum.

Silver Link Publishing Ltd
The Trundle
Ringstead Road
Great Addington
Kettering
Northants NN14 4BW

Tel/Fax: 01536 330588
email: sales@nostalgiacollection.com
Website: www.nostalgiacollection.com

Printed and bound in Česká Republika

OLD WARDEN The Garrett 1926 QL steam wagon poses in front of Shuttleworth House at the Bedfordshire Steam Rally in September 2004.

Traction engines

NORTH NIBLEY A 1920 Garrett traction engine at the Lister Tyndale Rally in June 2005.

STANWAY 1910 traction engine *Mercury* approaches Stanway in October 2003, heading for the Stanway Gala, and is seen later at Stanway House. This Gala was held for the last time in 2010.

BANBURY *Mercury* is seen again in June 1991 at the Banbury Steam Rally.

OLD WARDEN *Olive* a 1911 engine at the Bedfordshire Steam Rally in September 2003. This unusual engine carries a water superheater in the smokebox as can be clearly seen in the photograph.

HOLCOT This rally is no longer held, but in August 2001 the 1909 traction engine *Margaret* is about to be belted to a threshing box.

STONELEIGH PARK A 1909 engine at Stoneleigh Park Country Show in July 1992, another event that no longer takes place.

CF 3556

STOKE GOLDINGTON The same engine
is seen again at the Stoke Goldington Rally in
May 2002.

WEETING 1916 Garrett engine *Felstead Bell* at the Weeting Rally in Norfolk.

BIRMINGHAM Rallies around the centre of Birmingham based on the Museum of Science & Industry in Newhall Street, in the city's Jewellery Quarter, finished in the mid-1990s, and the museum moved to Aston. In May 1992 we see 1902 Garrett traction engine *Lucy*.

REDDITCH *Lucy* is the oldest Garrett traction engine in preservation, and is seen again in Davis's Yard, Astwood Bank, Redditch, in September 1992.

TARRANT HINTON Your author has only seen and photographed this rare beast once, in 1992, at the 'Great Dorset'. *The Joker* is a 1919 Garrett Suffolk Punch. This was the failed attempt by the firm to build a steam-driven tractor able to combat the petrol/diesel machines being made after the First World War.

BROADWAY *Lucy* on the road approaching Broadway in August 1998.

4CD steam tractors

EAST ANGLIA Taking part in the East Anglian Traction Engine Road Run in June 1997 is 1924 Garrett 4CD tractor *Evelyn*. The 4CDs were very well-liked engines.

DENNINGTON During the same event, *Evelyn* runs through Dennington village. Note the change of trailer.

ECTON PARK 1919 4CD *Horace* in action in August 1994 at the Ecton Park Rally, sadly no longer held.

OLD WARDEN *Horace* poses against the backdrop of Shuttleworth House during the Bedfordshire Steam Rally of September 1998.

STONELEIGH 1920 4CD KE 7124 passes spring blossom on a road run in May 2000.

STANWAY The same engine is seen in October the following year at the Gloucestershire Warwickshire Railway Steam & Vintage Gala at Stanway House.

WELLAND 1918 4CD tractor *Princess Mary* takes part in a road run from the rally site in July 2008.

Above: **STONELEIGH** A 1920 4CD poses in the village in May 2000

Opposite: **RUSHMOOR** The Rushmoor Rally is another that is no longer held, but in July 1998 played host to this 1919 4CD tractor.

Below: **ICKFORD** 1913 Garrett tractor *Mr Potter* hauls a water tanker at the Great Bucks Working Rally in July 2004.

Above: **STOKE ROW** At the Woodcote Rally at Greenaways Yard, Stoke Row, in July 2003 is a 1918 4CD in the livery of Wynn's Haulage (North Wales), a firm that did use traction engines in the early days.

LEIGHTON BUZZARD The Leighton
Buzzard Rally is now known as the St Albans
Rally, and one of the engines to be seen in May
2002 was 1921 4CD *Patricia*.

OLD WARDEN
The same engine is seen again at the Bedfordshire Steam Rally in September 2001.

BROMYARD A 1913 Garrett 4CD in the ring at the Bromyard Rally in July 1993.

PORTHTOWAN 1918 4CD tractor *Princess Mary* climbs Engine Hill, Porthtowan, Cornwall, during the West of England Steam Engine Society Road Run in August 1995.

TARRANT HINTON *Princess Mary* joins a line-up at the Great Dorset Steam Fair in September 1999.

Opposite: **HORRINGER** Running through the village during the East Anglia Road Run of May 2000 is 1918 4CD *Adventurer*.

Right: **STOKE ROW** 4CD *Dorothy* is photographed at the July 2003 rally.

Left: **WELLAND** A 1920 4CD at speed during the July 1999 rally.

WEETING Two 4CDs at the July 1992 rally:
a 1924 example in the parade ring *(below)*, and
1918 engine *Princess Royal*.

4CDS showman's engines

FRAMLINGHAM On an East Anglian Traction Engine Road run in May 1993 is 1918 4CDS showman's tractor *Lord George*. The 4CD tractor was popular with showmen and either came from the factory with showman's fittings, or they were fitted at a later date.

DENNINGTON *Lord George* approaches
Dennington village during the same run.

BANBURY 1918 Garrett
showman's tractor *Margaret* at
the Banbury Rally of June 1993.

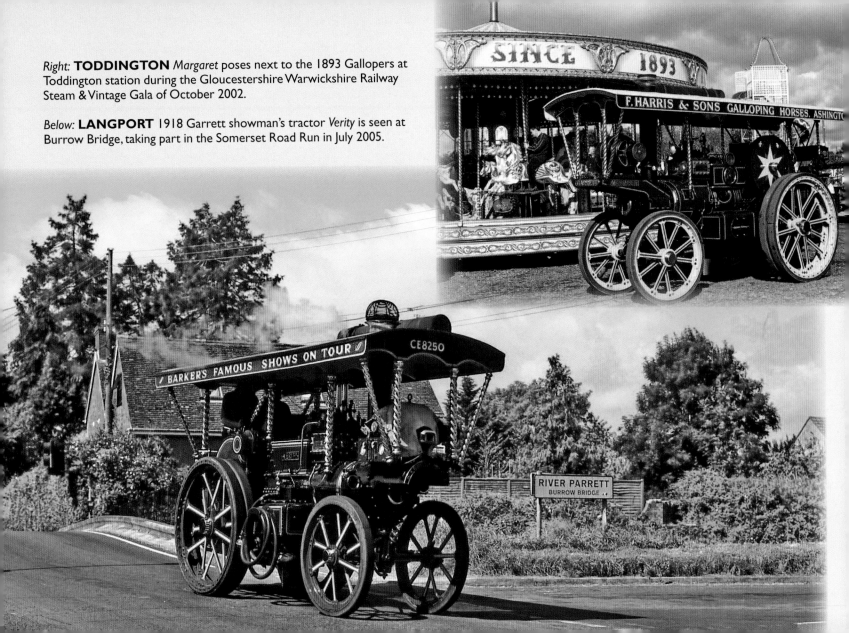

Right: **TODDINGTON** *Margaret* poses next to the 1893 Gallopers at Toddington station during the Gloucestershire Warwickshire Railway Steam & Vintage Gala of October 2002.

Below: **LANGPORT** 1918 Garrett showman's tractor *Verity* is seen at Burrow Bridge, taking part in the Somerset Road Run in July 2005.

BROMYARD 4CDS *Lady Sarah*, captured during the July 1991 Bromyard Rally.

DENNINGTON 1919 4CDS *Little Billy* enters the village while taking part in the East Anglian Traction Engine Road Run of May 1997.

OLD WARDEN Two views of *Little Billy* at the Bedfordshire Steam Rally.

TARRANT HINTON A Garrett showman's tractor lines up with the other fairground engines at the Great Dorset Steam Fair.

MUCH MARCLE
1919 4CDS *Queen of Great Britain* takes part in the Marcle Rally in July 2000.

Right: **KEMBLE** *Queen of Great Britain* is seen again at the Kemble Rally in August 2001, held since 2011 at South Cerney.

Below: **OLD WARDEN** 1918 Garrett showman's tractor *Bluebell*, at the Bedfordshire Steam Rally in September 2003.

RUSHMOOR 1917 4CDS *Countess* and her living van at the former Rushmoor Rally in July 1998.

Left: **UPTON ON SEVERN** This rally was the forerunner of the Welland Rally, and seen there in July 1991 is 1920 4CDS *The Leader.*

Below: **BANBURY** Another view of *The Leader* at the Banbury Rally of June 1993.

Bottom left: **BURBAGE** 1914 4CDS *The Greyhound* is seen at the Burbage Rally of June 1994.

Road locomotives

BANBURY 1908 Garret showman's road locomotive *British Hero* at work at the Banbury Rally in June 2002. While there are a number of showman's tractors preserved, only one showman's road locomotive is in preservation.

PETERSFIELD 1906 Garrett road locomotive *Vera* attends the July 1993 Downs Rally, an event that is no longer held. As with the showman's, only one road locomotive has been preserved.

PETERSFIELD *Vera* takes a demonstration heavy haulage load up the hill at the rally.

Road rollers

EAST ANGLIA Eight Garrett road rollers have been preserved, and here, taking part in the Great Eastern Road Run, is 1910 10-ton roller *Elizabeth*.

Cumberland County Council No.5, Keswick

Above: **WEETING** 1921 Garrett 10-ton road roller *The Baroness* stands at Weeting in July 1992. There are eight road rollers preserved

Left: **BRIXWORTH** *Elizabeth* is seen again on the National Traction Engine Trust 50th Road Run in Northamptonshire in August 1996.

DENNINGTON *The Baroness* runs through Dennington during the East Anglian Traction Engine Road Run in May 1993.

MUCH MARCLE *The Baroness* road roller was built in 1921 and is seen again at the Marcle Rally of July 2006.

Index